First Printing, 2017

Published by:
Lara Willing
www.larawilling.com

Cover by Tera Antaree

ISBN 978-0-692-93933-8

Take care of you!

♡ Lara

3 Things Journal

by Lara Willing

and YOU!

©Lara Willing 2017

I will be donating a portion of all proceeds
to the Human Awareness Institute (HAI Global)
to support the wonderful work
they do around the world and
to express my gratitude for
all the ways they have enriched my life.
www.HAI.org

Acknowledgements

To my clients, who inspire and teach me every day.

To my friends, family, and HAI community for all the ways you hold me.

To my closest circle - Michael, Mary, Christine, Margaret, Aaron, Todd, Lisa, Mike, and Barbara:
Thank you for being on this journey with me.

And, of course, to Gordo, who is and will be with me always.

Credits

Art by :

Anne E.G. Nydam

Christine Simpson

Claire Federico

Claudia Mariani

Cynthia Rolin Brown

Mariana Mesa

Michael Henley

Mindy Cutcher

Lara Willing

Cover design by Tera Antaree
Huge thanks to Tera for her patience
and precision with the cover and
proofreading!

Many of the art pieces were inspired by
the Zentangle Method.[a]

Credits

Writing by :

Quotes and poems are attributed to their author when known and are used with permission when appropriate.

All bullet point prompts, as well as unattributed quotes and tidbits are written by Lara Willing.

The interior font is Desyrel, created by Dana Rice

Welcome to your 3 Things Journal!

I invite you to use this journal to create a few minutes of self-care whenever you open it.

There are no rules or shoulds. You can use this journal however you want to!

Some people will diligently write in this journal every day. Others will read and write in it when they feel the urge.

Some will answer prompts with a word or two, others will use every bit of white space to write.

Some will skip around and find prompts they like. Others will look at only one page at a time and leave each new page to be a surprise.

The "Today is..." line can be filled in with a day or date, an adjective or anything else.

This journal is your space, to do with as you please. However you do it is perfect! Whatever you do, please don't use this as an(other?) opportunity to beat yourself up!

My hope is that your time with this journal will open your heart and your mind and give you an opportunity to reflect on your life. Most of all, I hope it feels good doing this for yourself. Happy journaling!

— Lara

Important tip:

You can get this journal spiral bound for just a few dollars at your local print shop. Then it will lie flat.

(Publishing it spiral bound is really expensive)

©Lara Willing 2017

Today is _____

3 things I am grateful for

-
-
-

3 beliefs I can let go of

-
-
-

3 things I promise myself

-
-
-

Today is _____

3 things I am excited about

-
-
-

3 things I have learned that
don't serve me

-
-
-

3 things I plan to do better

-
-
-

Today is _____

3 things I celebrate

-
-
-

3 things I want to stop doing

-
-
-

3 things that have changed my life

-
-
-

Run from what is
comfortable. Forget safety.
Live where you fear to live.
— Rumi

Today is _____

3 beautiful things I saw today
-
-
-

3 things I am working on changing
-
-
-

3 things I do often
-
-
-

Today is _____

3 ways others appreciate me

-
-
-

3 things that feel incomplete

-
-
-

3 things I will do for myself

-
-
-

Today is _____

3 things I smile about

-
-
-

3 mistakes I have learned from

-
-
-

3 risks I am willing to take

-
-
-

I am only one,
but I am one.
I can not do
everything, but I
can do
something.
I must not fail
to do the
something that
I can do.

— Edward Everett Hale

Today is _____

3 things I treasure

-
-
-

3 things I regret

-
-
-

3 things I am managing well

-
-
-

Today is _____

3 things people like about me

-
-
-

3 things I am confused about

-
-
-

3 ways I make the world a
better place

-
-
-

Today is _____

3 things I do well

-
-
-

3 things I want to get better at

-
-
-

3 ways I challenge myself

-
-
-

Three things I have learned at HAI workshops:

- People are much more like me than they are different from me.
- We all hunger for love, touch, empathy, and connection. And we can create it.
- How to listen with my heart and how good it feels to be seen and heard.

— Lara Willing

The Human Awareness Institute
www.HAI.org
since 1968

Today is _____

3 ways I give to myself

-
-
-

3 things I want to stop doing

-
-
-

3 things I want to forgive

-
-
-

Today is _____

3 ways I have fun

-
-
-

3 ways I sabotage myself

-
-
-

3 ways I take care of myself

-
-
-

Today is _____

3 things I am optimistic about

-
-
-

3 things I have learned that don't serve me

-
-
-

3 things I plan to do better

-
-
-

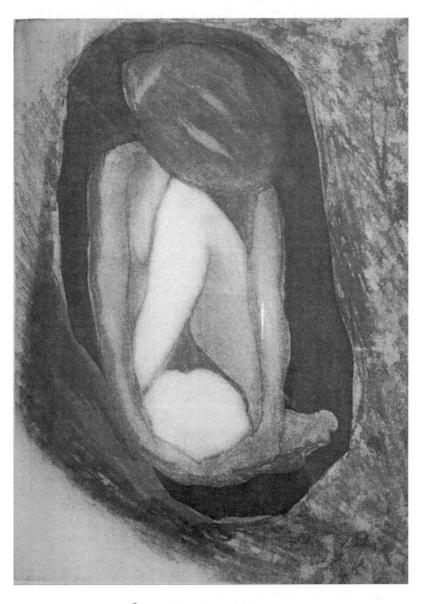

©Cynthia Rolin Brown

When I live in my heart, I am always home.

Today is _____

3 things I accomplished

-
-
-

3 things I feel guilty about

-
-
-

3 things I can do when I'm
feeling down

-
-
-

Today is _____

3 ways I prioritize me

-
-
-

3 things that feel incomplete

-
-
-

3 things I want more of

-
-
-

Today is _____

3 things I am grateful for

-
-
-

3 things I stand up against

-
-
-

3 things that have changed
my life

-
-
-

How could anyone ever tell you
You were anything less than
beautiful?

How could anyone ever tell you
You were less than whole?

How could anyone fail to notice
That your loving is a miracle?

How deeply you're
connected to my soul?

Today is _____

3 things I care about

-
-
-

3 things I want to change
about my life

-
-
-

3 things I got done today

-
-
-

Today is _____

3 good deeds I have done

-
-
-

3 ways I touch people's lives

-
-
-

3 things I forgive myself for

-
-
-

Today is _____

3 things I am content with

-
-
-

3 things I want to change

-
-
-

3 things I need help with

-
-
-

You are nothing short of a miracle. The precious incarnation that is you had a probability of

1 in 400,000,000,000,000 chance

of being born. And that doesn't even account for the unique experiences that have molded who you are right now.

Live and love like the miracle you are.

Today is _____

3 things I am happy about

-

-

-

3 ways I could try harder

-

-

-

3 things I will do to make
tomorrow better

-

-

-

Today is _____

3 things I am passionate about

-
-
-

3 things I feel defensive about

-
-
-

3 ways I help those I love

-
-
-

Today is _____

3 things I am confident about

-
-
-

3 things I resist

-
-
-

3 things I am satisfied with

-
-
-

©Claudia Mariani

The wound is the place
where the light enters you.
Stay with it.
— Rumi

Today is _____

3 beliefs I hold dear

-
-
-

3 values I live by

-
-
-

3 things I promise

-
-
-

Today is _____

3 things I am proud of

-
-
-

3 things I feel guilty about

-
-
-

3 things I want to do better

-
-
-

Today is _____

3 things I like just how
they are

-
-
-

3 things I say no to

-
-
-

3 things I am focusing on

-
-
-

Suffering $=$ wanting things to be different than they are

Today is _____

3 things I feel warm and
cozy about

-
-
-

3 ways I touch people's lives

-
-
-

3 things I forgive myself for

-
-
-

Today is _____

3 things I want

-
-
-

3 things I don't want

-
-
-

3 ways I am moving forward

-
-
-

Today is _____

3 things I commend myself for

-
-
-

3 things I want to stop doing

-
-
-

3 things I can give

-
-
-

A+!

Great work!

Today is _____

3 things I like about my body

-
-
-

3 ways I take care of myself

-
-
-

3 things I struggle with

-
-
-

Today is _____

3 things I have integrity about

-
-
-

3 things that confuse me

-
-
-

3 things I resisted today

-
-
-

Today is _____

3 insights I have had

-
-
-

3 things I attract to me

-
-
-

3 ways I treat others well

-
-
-

©Lara Willing

Life is a series of experiences...
leading nowhere.
Welcome to NOW!
— Peter Rengel

Today is _____

3 things that bring me
pleasure

-
-
-

3 ways I deny myself

-
-
-

3 things I am good at

-
-
-

Today is _____

3 things that inspire me

-
-
-

3 ways I could treat
myself better

-
-
-

3 ways I challenge myself

-
-
-

Today is _____

3 ways I have been brave

-
-
-

3 ways I touch people's lives

-
-
-

3 ways I am a good friend

-
-
-

Living in alignment with our own values is success. Let your values alone guide your striving.
— Lara Willing

Some Common Core Values		
Authenticity	Boldness	Compassion
Engagement	Cooperation	Trust
Integrity	Honesty	Ambition
Beauty	Generosity	Creativity
Balance	Autonomy	Faith
Fairness	Fun	Growth
Happiness	Family	Knowledge
Leadership	Competence	Humor
Influence	Education	Peace
Pleasure	Trust	Spirituality
Athleticism	Individuality	Respect
Poise	Loyalty	Love
Service	Curiosity	Challenge
Achievement	Community	Strength
Contribution	Charity	Stability
Courage	Security	Adventure
Change	Innovation	Connection

Today is _____

3 good deeds I have done

-
-
-

3 ways I touch people's lives

-
-
-

3 things I am good at

-
-
-

Today is _____

3 things that make me
come alive

-
-
-

3 things I want to stop doing

-
-
-

3 things I am accepting

-
-
-

Today is _____

3 ways I shine

-
-
-

3 ways I am healing

-
-
-

3 things I do for my family/
community/tribe

-
-
-

Intimacy is a basic human need, as much as food, water, and shelter. Intimacy is both vulnerable and powerful.
It takes courage to allow your inner self to be seen by another.

Intimacy = into me you see

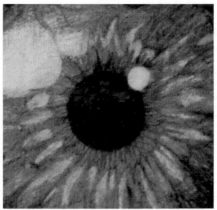

photo credit artxplorez.com

Today is _____

3 times I laughed today

-
-
-

3 things I wish were different

-
-
-

3 ways I am playful

-
-
-

Today is _____

3 things I have accomplished

-
-
-

3 things I struggle with

-
-
-

3 things I feel good about

-
-
-

Today is _____

3 values I live by

-
-
-

3 ways I let myself down

-
-
-

3 things I promise

-
-
-

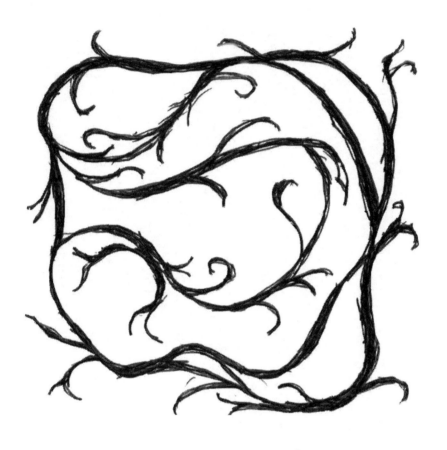

©Claire Federico

Sharing your art is inviting
others into your own private
conversation with yourself.

Today is _____

3 ways I am thriving

-

-

-

3 healthy habits I am building

-

-

-

3 ways I focus on me

-

-

-

Today is _____

3 things I am passionate about

-
-
-

3 things that irk me

-
-
-

3 things that come easily
to me

-
-
-

Today is _____

3 wonderful things I
absolutely deserve

-
-
-

3 ways I want to grow

-
-
-

3 things I can relax about

-
-
-

Draw what you feel right now

Today is _____

3 dreams I have

-

-

-

3 of my rules for living

-

-

-

3 things that show I have a
good life

-

-

-

Today is _____

3 people who have had an
impact on my life

-
-
-

3 things that don't serve me

-
-
-

3 opportunities I will seek out

-
-
-

Today is _____

3 things I am looking forward to

-
-
-

3 things I say no to

-
-
-

3 ways I build myself up

-
-
-

If you think you are too
small to make a difference,
try sleeping with a mosquito.
— Dalai Lama XIV

Today is _____

3 things that inspire me

-
-
-

3 things I want to change

-
-
-

3 ways I know I matter

-
-
-

Today is _____

3 things I am thrilled by

-
-
-

3 ways I limit myself

-
-
-

3 beliefs I hold dear

-
-
-

Today is _____

3 things I completely accept

-
-
-

3 things that matter to me

-
-
-

3 things I am ready to
leave behind

-
-
-

Although the world is full of suffering, it is full also of the overcoming of it.
— Helen Keller

Today is _____

3 ways I center myself

-

-

-

3 things I want to stop doing

-

-

-

3 things I am getting better at

-

-

-

Today is _____

3 things I like to do

-
-
-

3 things I am learning about

-
-
-

3 ways I honor myself

-
-
-

Today is _____

3 things I like about my body

-
-
-

3 ways I have room to grow

-
-
-

3 things I have overcome

-
-
-

Try this practice:

Take a conscious breath and roll your shoulders.

Congratulations! You just meditated.

Repeat as needed.

Today is _____

3 things that make me smile

-
-
-

3 ways I feel stuck

-
-
-

3 things I am focusing on

-
-
-

Today is _____

3 things that energize me

-
-
-

3 ways I used my body today

-
-
-

3 things I did well today

-
-
-

Today is _____

3 things others appreciate
about me

-
-
-

3 things I want to do more of

-
-
-

3 things I care about

-
-
-

We can complain
that rose bushes
have thorns,
or rejoice that
thorn bushes have roses.
— Abraham Lincoln
(unverified author)

Today is _____

3 ways I am a good friend

-
-
-

3 things I could do better

-
-
-

3 things I wish I could
do again

-
-
-

Today is _____

3 things that thrill me

-
-
-

3 things I wish I hadn't done

-
-
-

3 things I look for in a friend

-
-
-

Today is _____

3 things I take pride in

-
-
-

3 things I stand up for

-
-
-

3 ways I am creative

-
-
-

A bird
sitting in a tree is
not afraid of the
branch breaking.
Her trust is
not on the branch but
on her own wings.

— Unknown

Today is _____

3 things I feel eager about

-
-
-

3 things that are good for me

-
-
-

3 ways I exercise my mind

-
-
-

Today is _____

3 ways I get along well with others

-
-
-

3 ways I make a difference

-
-
-

3 things I will look for

-
-
-

Today is _____

3 things I feel lucky to have

-
-
-

3 ways I touch people's lives

-
-
-

3 ways I have grown

-
-
-

©Michael Henley

"Pain is inevitable.
Suffering is optional."

Today is _____

3 things I love

-
-
-

3 things I worry about

-
-
-

3 important steps I have taken

-
-
-

Today is _____

3 things that have changed
my life

-
-
-

3 ways I show I care

-
-
-

3 things I am good at

-
-
-

Today is _____

3 ways I am blessed

-
-
-

3 ways I give back

-
-
-

3 ways I include myself

-
-
-

Your task is not to seek for love, but merely to seek and find all the barriers within yourself that you have built against it.

— Rumi

Today is _____

3 things I accomplished today

-
-
-

3 things I struggle with

-
-
-

3 things that I enjoy

-
-
-

Today is _____

3 ways I excel

-
-
-

3 ways I challenge myself

-
-
-

3 things I want for others

-
-
-

Today is _____

3 things I feel good about

-
-
-

3 things I could do better

-
-
-

3 ways I am growing

-
-
-

Live as if you were to
die tomorrow.

Learn as if you were to
live forever.

Love as if you had
nothing to lose.

— adapted from
Mahatma Gandhi

Today is _____

3 ways I stretch myself

-
-
-

3 things I overlook

-
-
-

3 simple things that matter

-
-
-

Today is _____

3 things I get excited about

-
-
-

3 ways I treat myself well

-
-
-

3 things I know for sure

-
-
-

Today is _____

3 ways I am a good friend

-
-
-

3 ways I keep life simple

-
-
-

3 things I want more of

-
-
-

The Human Awareness Institute produces workshops on Love, Intimacy, and Sexuality.

For me, the workshops are really about Trust, Honesty and Communication. In other words, being human with others.

When you take a HAI workshop, you connect more deeply with yourself and with a thriving, loving community.

I recommend HAI workshops without hesitation.

— Lara Willing

The Human Awareness Institute
www.HAI.org

Today is _____

3 ways I prioritize pleasure

-

-

-

3 ways I hold myself back

-

-

-

3 things people appreciate about me

-

-

-

Today is _____

3 things I want to do more of

-
-
-

3 things I want to learn about

-
-
-

3 ways I have fun

-
-
-

Today is _____

3 ways my life has improved

-
-
-

3 ways I let myself down

-
-
-

3 things I know a lot about

-
-
-

©Lara Willing

If you are in a bad mood, go for a walk. If you are still in a bad mood, go for another walk.

— Hippocrates

Today is _____

3 things I can do today to
make tomorrow go better

-
-
-

3 beliefs I can let go of

-
-
-

3 things I promise myself

-
-
-

Today is _____

3 ways I center myself

-
-
-

3 things I have learned that don't serve me

-
-
-

3 things I plan to do better

-
-
-

Today is _____

3 things I celebrate

-
-
-

3 things I want to stop doing

-
-
-

3 things that have changed
my life

-
-
-

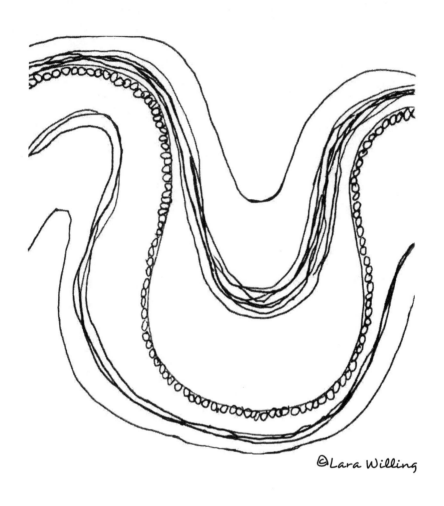

©Lara Willing

You can't stop the waves, but
you can learn to surf.
— Jon Kabat-Zinn

Today is _____

3 beautiful things around me
-
-
-

3 things I wish I could do over
again differently
-
-
-

3 things I look forward to
-
-
-

Today is _____

3 ways others show they
appreciate me

-
-
-

3 things that feel incomplete

-
-
-

3 things I will do for myself

-
-
-

Today is _____

3 things I smile about

-
-
-

3 mistakes I have learned from

-
-
-

3 risks I am willing to take

-
-
-

Change will not come if we wait for some other person or some other time. We are the ones we've been waiting for. We are the change that we seek.

— Barack Obama

Today is _____

3 things I treasure

-
-
-

3 things I regret

-
-
-

3 things I am working toward

-
-
-

Today is _____

3 things people like about me

-
-
-

3 things I am confused about

-
-
-

3 ways I make the world a
better place

-
-
-

Today is _____

3 things I do well

-
-
-

3 things I want to get better at

-
-
-

3 ways I challenge myself

-
-
-

When you are in the light,
soak it all up so you can
take it into the dark
with you.

Today is _____

3 ways I give to myself

-

-

-

3 things I want to stop doing

-

-

-

3 things I want to think about more

-

-

-

Today is _____

3 ways I have fun

-
-
-

3 ways I sabotage myself

-
-
-

3 ways I take care of myself

-
-
-

Today is _____

3 things I am positive about

-
-
-

3 things I have learned that
don't serve me

-
-
-

3 things I plan to do better

-
-
-

now!

This is the perfect place at the perfect time.
You are right where you need to be.

Today is _____

3 things I accomplished

-
-
-

3 things I feel guilty about

-
-
-

3 things I intend to do better

-
-
-

Today is _____

3 ways I prioritize me

-
-
-

3 things that feel incomplete

-
-
-

3 things I want more of

-
-
-

Today is _____

3 things I am grateful for

-
-
-

3 things I stand up against

-
-
-

3 things that have changed
my life

-
-
-

©Lara Willing

I do not understand the
mystery of grace — only that
it meets us where we are and
does not leave us where it
found us.

— Anne Lamott

Today is _____

3 things I care about

-
-
-

3 things I want to change about my life

-
-
-

3 things I got done today

-
-
-

Today is _____

3 good deeds I have done

-

-

-

3 ways I touch people's lives

-

-

-

3 things I need help with

-

-

-

Today is _____

3 things I am content with

-
-
-

3 things I want to change

-
-
-

3 things I am good at

-
-
-

Hugs are good for you:

- They boost oxytocin (the cuddle and love hormone).
- They reduce cortisol (the stress hormone).
- They enhance trust and closeness.
- They feel good!

How to hug:

Be present for your hugs.

Start with eye contact and make sure you have permission.

Place your hearts together and take a breath or two like that.

As you pull away, say good bye with your eyes.

Today is _____

3 things I am happy about

-
-
-

3 ways I could try harder

-
-
-

3 things I will do for myself

-
-
-

Today is _____

3 things I am passionate about

-
-
-

3 things I feel defensive about

-
-
-

3 ways I help

-
-
-

Today is _____

3 things I am optimistic about

-
-
-

3 things I resist

-
-
-

3 things I am satisfied with

-
-
-

Would you rather
wish you had or
wish you hadn't?

Today is _____

3 beliefs I hold dear

-
-
-

3 values I live by

-
-
-

3 things I promise

-
-
-

Today is _____

3 things I am attracted to

-
-
-

3 things I feel guilty about

-
-
-

3 things I stand by

-
-
-

Today is _____

3 things I like just as they are

-
-
-

3 things I say no to

-
-
-

3 things I am starting

-
-
-

If you want to have
something different than
you've ever had,
you have to do
something different than
you've ever done.

— Thomas Jefferson

Today is _____

3 things I feel warm and
cozy about

-
-
-

3 ways I touch people's lives

-
-
-

3 things I forgive myself for

-
-
-

Today is _____

3 things I want

-
-
-

3 things I don't want

-
-
-

3 ways I am moving forward

-
-
-

Today is _____

3 things I commend
myself for

-
-
-

3 things I want to stop doing

-
-
-

3 things I have to give

-
-
-

Remember always that you
not only have the right to be
an individual, you have an
obligation to be one.
— Eleanor Roosevelt

Today is _____

3 ways I connect
authentically

-
-
-

3 ways I take care of myself

-
-
-

3 things I struggle with

-
-
-

Today is _____

3 things I have integrity about

-
-
-

3 things that confuse me

-
-
-

3 things I resisted today

-
-
-

Today is _____

3 insights I have had

-
-
-

3 things I home in on

-
-
-

3 ways I treat others well

-
-
-

©Lara Willing

That it will never come again
is what makes life so sweet.
— Emily Dickinson

Today is _____

3 things that bring me pleasure

-
-
-

3 ways I deny myself

-
-
-

3 things I am good at

-
-
-

Today is _____

3 things that inspire me

-
-
-

3 ways I could treat
myself better

-
-
-

3 ways I challenge myself

-
-
-

Today is _____

3 ways I have been brave

-
-
-

3 ways I touch people's lives

-
-
-

3 ways I am a good friend

-
-
-

Seeking pleasure, gratitude, and beauty is better for your soul (and your relationships) than focusing on what is lacking.

Pay attention to the 95% that works instead of the 5% that doesn't.

Today is _____

3 good deeds I have done

-
-
-

3 ways I show up

-
-
-

3 things I am working on

-
-
-

Today is _____

3 things that make me come
alive

-
-
-

3 things I want to stop doing

-
-
-

3 things I am good at

-
-
-

Today is _____

3 ways I shine

-
-
-

3 ways I am healing

-
-
-

3 things I do for my family/
community/tribe

-
-
-

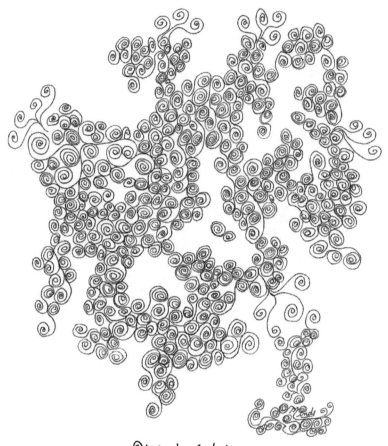

©Mindy Cutcher

You are not
a drop in the ocean.
You are
the entire ocean in a drop.
— Rumi

Today is _____

3 times I laughed today

-
-
-

3 things I wish were different

-
-
-

3 ways I play

-
-
-

Today is _____

3 things I have accomplished

-
-
-

3 things I struggle with

-
-
-

3 things I feel good about

-
-
-

Today is _____

3 values I live by

-
-
-

3 ways I let myself down

-
-
-

3 things I promise

-
-
-

©Mariana Mesa

Connecting with ourselves first
helps us connect with the world
from a quieter,
more peaceful place inside.

Today is _____

3 ways I am thriving

-
-
-

3 healthy habits I am
building

-
-
-

3 ways I focus on me

-
-
-

Today is _____

3 things I am passionate about

-
-
-

3 things that irk me

-
-
-

3 things that serve me today

-
-
-

Today is _____

3 wonderful things I
absolutely deserve

-
-
-

3 ways I want to grow

-
-
-

3 things I can relax about

-
-
-

Confucius said:

To practice five things under all circumstances constitutes perfect virtue.

These five things are:
  - gravity
    - generosity of soul
      - sincerity
        - earnestness, and
        - kindness

(What do you think?)

Today is _____

3 dreams I have

-
-
-

3 of my rules for living

-
-
-

3 things that show I have a
good life

-
-
-

Today is _____

3 people who have had an
impact on my life

-
-
-

3 things that don't serve me

-
-
-

3 opportunities I will seek out

-
-
-

Today is _____

3 things I am looking
forward to

-
-
-

3 things I say no to

-
-
-

3 ways I build myself up

-
-
-

©Christine M Simpson

Today is _____

3 things that inspire me

-
-
-

3 things I want to change

-
-
-

3 ways I know I matter

-
-
-

Today is _____

3 things I am thrilled by

-
-
-

3 ways I limit myself

-
-
-

3 beliefs I hold dear

-
-
-

Today is _____

3 things I completely accept

-
-
-

3 things that matter to me

-
-
-

3 things I am ready to
leave behind

-
-
-

Resist comparing your insides to other people's outsides. You are seeing only the parts they want you to see.

Assume instead that people are much more like you than different from you. We all love, hurt, dream, fear, and yearn.

What if we are all perfect in our magnificence and our fragility?

— Lara Willing

Today is _____

3 things I am enthusiastic
about

-
-
-

3 things I want to stop doing

-
-
-

3 things I am getting better at

-
-
-

Today is _____

3 things I like

-
-
-

3 things I am learning about

-
-
-

3 ways I honor myself

-
-
-

Today is _____

3 things I like about my body

-
-
-

3 ways I have room to grow

-
-
-

3 things I have worked toward

-
-
-

Open your hands
if you want to be held.
— Rumi

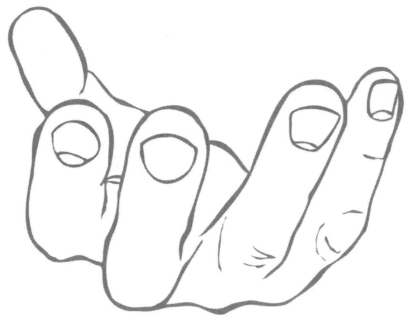

Today is _____

3 things that make me smile

-
-
-

3 ways I feel stuck

-
-
-

3 things I am focusing on

-
-
-

Today is _____

3 things that energize me

-
-
-

3 ways I used my body today

-
-
-

3 things I did well today

-
-
-

Today is _____

3 things others appreciate
about me

-
-
-

3 things I want to do more of

-
-
-

3 things I care about

-
-
-

The sturdiest tree is not found
in the shelter of the forest
but high upon some rocky crag,
where its daily battle with the
elements shapes it into
a thing of beauty.
— Unknown

Today is _____

3 ways I am a good friend

-
-
-

3 things I could do better

-
-
-

3 things I like about myself

-
-
-

Today is _____

3 things that thrill me

-
-
-

3 things I wish I hadn't done

-
-
-

3 things I look for in a friend

-
-
-

Today is _____

3 things I am proud of

-
-
-

3 things I stand up for

-
-
-

3 ways I am creative

-
-
-

©Lara Willing

We might as well
think big
since we have to
think anyway.

Today is _____

3 things I feel eager about

-
-
-

3 things that are good for me

-
-
-

3 ways I exercise my mind

-
-
-

Today is _____

3 ways I get along well
with others

-
-
-

3 ways I make a difference

-
-
-

3 things I will look for

-
-
-

Today is _____

3 things I feel lucky to have

-
-
-

3 ways I touch people's lives

-
-
-

3 ways I have grown

-
-
-

I participated in my first HAI workshop in 1995 and felt like I had come home and found my chosen family.

I am grateful every day for the amazing, heart-opening work that this organization does.

— Lara Willing

The Human Awareness Institute
www.HAI.org

Today is _____

3 things I love

-
-
-

3 things I worry about

-
-
-

3 important steps I have taken

-
-
-

Today is _____

3 things that have changed
my life

-
-
-

3 ways I show I care

-
-
-

3 things I am good at

-
-
-

Today is _____

3 ways I am blessed

-
-
-

3 ways I give back

-
-
-

3 things I am a part of

-
-
-

You have everything you need
to take this next step.

Today is _____

3 things I accomplished today

-
-
-

3 things I struggle with

-
-
-

3 things that I enjoy

-
-
-

Today is _____

3 ways I excel

-
-
-

3 ways I challenge myself

-
-
-

3 things I want for others

-
-
-

Today is _____

3 things I feel good about

-
-
-

3 things I could do better

-
-
-

3 ways I am growing

-
-
-

It all changed when I realized I'm not the only one on the planet who's scared. Everyone else is, too.

— Stan Dale (founder of HAI)

Today is _____

3 ways I stretch myself

-
-
-

3 things I overlook

-
-
-

3 simple things that matter

-
-
-

Today is _____

3 things I feel confident about

-
-
-

3 ways I treat myself well

-
-
-

3 things I know for sure

-
-
-

Today is _____

3 ways I am a good partner/
friend/parent

- •
- •
- •

3 ways I keep life simple

- •
- •
- •

3 things I want more of

- •
- •
- •

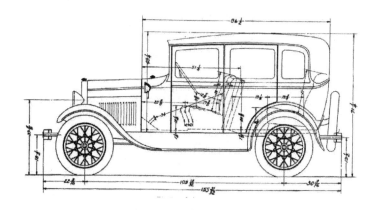

Whether you think you can or
think you can't, you're right.

— Henry Ford

Today is _____

3 ways I will seek out beauty

-

-

-

3 ways I hold myself back

-

-

-

3 things people appreciate
about me

-

-

-

Today is _____

3 things I want to do more of

-
-
-

3 things I want to learn about

-
-
-

3 ways I have fun

-
-
-

Today is _____

3 ways I promise to be good
to myself

-
-
-

3 ways I let myself down

-
-
-

3 things I know a lot about

-
-
-

your love is enough

Today is _____

3 things that made me smile
today

-
-
-

3 ways I feel stuck

-
-
-

3 things I long for

-
-
-

Today is _____

3 things that energize me

-
-
-

3 ways I used my body today

-
-
-

3 things I did well today

-
-
-

Today is _____

3 things others appreciate me for

-
-
-

3 things I want to do more of

-
-
-

3 things I care about

-
-
-

Good morning, sweetheart,
I will be taking care of
everything for you today.
There is nothing you need to
worry about. I've got this!
Go out and have a good time.

Love, The Universe

Today is _____

3 ways I am a good friend

-
-
-

3 things I could do better

-
-
-

3 things I like about myself

-
-
-

Today is _____

3 things that thrill me

- •

- •

- •

3 things I wish I hadn't done today

- •

- •

- •

3 things I look for in a friend

- •

- •

- •

Today is _____

3 things I am attracted to

-
-
-

3 things I stand up for

-
-
-

3 ways I am creative

-
-
-

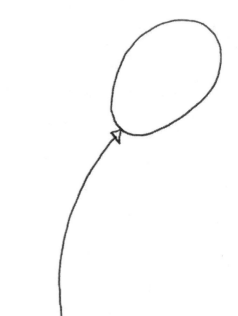

Forgiveness is letting go of hope for a different past.

Today is _____

3 things I feel eager about

-
-
-

3 things that are good for me

-
-
-

3 ways I exercise my mind

-
-
-

Today is _____

3 ways I get along well
with others

-
-
-

3 ways I make a difference

-
-
-

3 things I will look for

-
-
-

Today is _____

3 things I feel lucky to have

-

-

-

3 ways I touch people's lives

-

-

-

3 ways I have grown

-

-

-

Don't believe everything
you think.

Make it a practice to assume
there are other explanations.

Today is _____

3 things I love

-
-
-

3 things I worry about

-
-
-

3 important steps I have taken

-
-
-

Today is _____

3 things that have changed
my life

-
-
-

3 ways I show I care

-
-
-

3 things I am good at

-
-
-

Today is _____

3 ways I am blessed

-
-
-

3 ways I give back

-
-
-

3 things I am a part of

-
-
-

Draw what you feel right now

Today is _____

3 things I accomplished today

-

-

-

3 things I struggle with

-

-

-

3 things that I enjoy

-

-

-

Today is _____

3 ways I excel

-
-
-

3 ways I challenge myself

-
-
-

3 things I want for others

-
-
-

Today is _____

3 things I feel optimistic about

-
-
-

3 things I could do better

-
-
-

3 ways I am growing

-
-
-

Try this practice:

Scrunch up your face as tight
as you can. Tighten your
mouth, your eyes, your nose
— hold it —
then open your mouth and
your face as big as you can,
like a lion roaring.

What do you notice?

Today is _____

3 things I am grateful for

-
-
-

3 beliefs I can let go of

-
-
-

3 ways I am nice to my
future self

-
-
-

Today is _____

3 things I am planning for

-
-
-

3 things I have learned that
don't serve me

-
-
-

3 things I hope to improve

-
-
-

Today is _____

3 things I celebrate

-
-
-

3 things I want to stop doing

-
-
-

3 things that have changed
my life

-
-
-

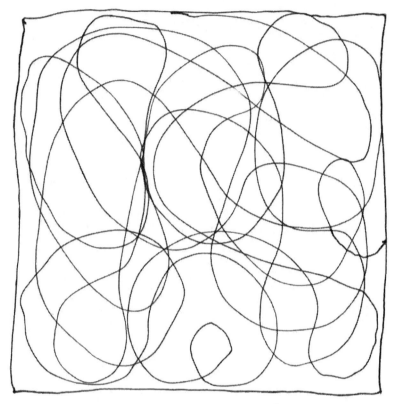

©Lara Willing

chaos is perfect.

Today is _____

3 beautiful things I saw today
-
-
-

3 things I wish I'd started sooner
-
-
-

3 things I feel confident about
-
-
-

Today is _____

3 ways others appreciate me

-

-

-

3 things that feel incomplete

-

-

-

3 things I will do for myself

-

-

-

Today is _____

3 things I smile about

-
-
-

3 lessons I have learned

-
-
-

3 risks I am willing to take

-
-
-

©Lara Willing

Forever is composed of nows.
— Emily Dickinson

Today is _____

3 things I treasure

-
-
-

3 things I regret

-
-
-

3 things I am working toward

-
-
-

Today is _____

3 things people like about me

-
-
-

3 things I forgive myself for

-
-
-

3 ways I make the world a
better place

-
-
-

Today is _____

3 things I do well

-
-
-

3 things I want to get better at

-
-
-

3 ways I challenge myself

-
-
-

Three things I learned at HAI workshops:

- The unknown can be exciting instead of scary.
- Healing my relationship with my body and my sexuality is possible.
- We all share similar joys, fears, longings, and hurts.

— Lara Willing

The Human Awareness Institute
www.HAI.org

Today is _____

3 ways I give to myself

-
-
-

3 things I want to stop doing

-
-
-

3 things I want to think
about more

-
-
-

Today is _____

3 ways I have fun

-
-
-

3 ways I sabotage myself

-
-
-

3 things I can do today to
make tomorrow better

-
-
-

Today is _____

3 things I am drawn to

-
-
-

3 things I have learned that
don't serve me

-
-
-

3 ways I take care of myself

-
-
-

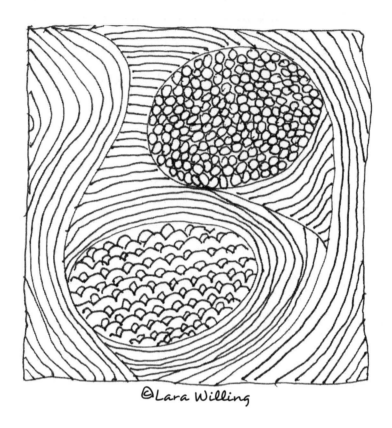

©Lara Willing

The past is gone.
Do not worship it.

The future hasn't happened yet.
Do not dwell there.

The present is a gift.
Open it, throw away the box,
and enjoy!

— Lara Willing

Today is _____

3 things I accomplished

-
-
-

3 things I feel guilty about

-
-
-

3 things I intend to do better

-
-
-

Today is _____

3 ways I prioritize me

-
-
-

3 things that feel incomplete

-
-
-

3 things I want more of

-
-
-

Today is _____

3 things I am grateful for

-
-
-

3 things I stand up against

-
-
-

3 things that have changed
my life

-
-
-

your lifelong
companion

This, above all else:
to thine own self be true.
— William Shakespeare

Thank you for including me and the **3 Things Journal** on your self-care journey. My sincere hope is that this journal has led to introspection that has enhanced your self-awareness and increased your compassion for yourself.

I encourage you to make yourself and your self-care a priority despite the pull of work, family, health or logistics. Put on your own oxygen mask first.

I wish for you a glorious balance of connection, joy, adventure, tenderness, and growth. And I believe you can have it _all_!

With care,

Lara

Lara Willing 2017 ©